Pope

Give yourself
to Christ

First Homilies of Benedict XVI

*All booklets are published thanks to the
generous support of the members of the
Catholic Truth Society*

CATHOLIC TRUTH SOCIETY
PUBLISHERS TO THE HOLY SEE

'If we let Christ into our lives, we lose nothing, nothing, absolutely nothing of what makes life free, beautiful and great. No! Only in this friendship are the doors of life opened wide. Only in this friendship is the great potential of human existence truly revealed. Only in this friendship do we experience beauty and liberation'. - Homily, Inaugural Mass, St Peter's Square, 24 April 2005.

Contents

4

Introduction

The passing of one Pope and the election of a successor are events that combine to form a momentous few weeks in the life of the Catholic Church - and, as the events of April 2005 have illustrated, even beyond to a wider audience. The death of Pope John Paul II and the election of Pope Benedict XVI have certainly raised the interest of millions around the globe.

This collection of homilies given by Cardinal Joseph Ratzinger during the period between the death of John Paul II, and his own election and inauguration as Pope Benedict XVI, capture the sentiments and aspirations not only of one man, or of the College of Cardinals, but the aspirations and prayers of a whole people.

These brief and clear texts express the overwhelming reliance the Christian must place upon scripture, the Word of God, and prayer; they relate the Christian search to discern the will of God, and above all, crystallize something of the thought and spirit of this new successor of St Peter - Benedict XVI, the Good Shepherd, the Good Fisherman.

- *Easter, 2005*

'My real programme ... is not to do my own will, not to pursue my own ideas, but to listen, together with the whole Church, to the word and the will of the Lord, to be guided by Him, so that He himself will lead the Church at this hour of our history.' - Homily, Inaugural Mass, St Peter's Square, 24 April 2005.

1. Homily of His Eminence Cardinal Joseph Ratzinger, Dean of the College of Cardinals, during the Funeral Mass of the Roman Pontiff John Paul II

St Peter's Square Friday, 8 April 2005

"Follow me." The Risen Lord says these words to Peter. They are his last words to this disciple, chosen to shepherd his flock. "Follow me" - this lapidary saying of Christ can be taken as the key to understanding the message which comes to us from the life of our late beloved Pope John Paul II. Today we bury his remains in the earth as a seed of immortality - our hearts are full of sadness, yet at the same time of joyful hope and profound gratitude.

These are the sentiments that inspire us, brothers and sisters in Christ, present here in St. Peter's Square, in neighboring streets and in various other locations within the city of Rome, where an immense crowd, silently praying, has gathered over the last few days. I greet all of you from my heart. In the name of the College of Cardinals, I also wish to express my respects to heads of state, heads of government and the delegations from various countries.

I greet the authorities and official representatives of other Churches and Christian Communities, and likewise those of different religions. Next I greet the archbishops, bishops, priests, religious men and women and the faithful who have come here from every continent; especially the young, whom John Paul II liked to call the future and the hope of the Church. My greeting is extended, moreover, to all those throughout the world who are united with us through radio and television in this solemn celebration of our beloved Holy Father's funeral.

Follow me - as a young student Karol Wojtyla was thrilled by literature, the theater and poetry. Working in a chemical plant, surrounded and threatened by the Nazi terror, he heard the voice of the Lord: Follow me! In this extraordinary setting he began to read books of philosophy and theology, and then entered the clandestine seminary established by Cardinal Sapieha. After the war he was able to complete his studies in the faculty of theology of the Jagiellonian University of Krakow.

How often, in his letters to priests and in his autobiographical books, has he spoken to us about his priesthood, to which he was ordained on November 1, 1946. In these texts he interprets his priesthood with particular reference to three sayings of the Lord.

First: "It was not you who chose me, but I who chose you and appointed you to go and bear fruit that will remain" (*John* 15:16). The second saying is: "A good shepherd lays down his life for the sheep" (*John* 10:11). And then: "As the Father loves me, so I also love you. Remain in my love" (*John* 15:9). In these three sayings we see the heart and soul of our Holy Father. He really went everywhere, untiringly, in order to bear fruit, fruit that lasts.

"*Rise, Let Us Be on Our Way!*" is the title of his next-to-last book. "Rise, let us be on our way!" - with these words he roused us from a lethargic faith, from the sleep of the disciples of both yesterday and today. "Rise, let us be on our way!" he continues to say to us even today. The Holy Father was a priest to the last, for he offered his life to God for his flock and for the entire human family, in a daily self-oblation for the service of the Church, especially amid the sufferings of his final months. And in this way he became one with Christ, the Good Shepherd who loves his sheep.

Finally, "abide in my love": The Pope who tried to meet everyone, who had an ability to forgive and to open his heart to all, tells us once again today, with these words of the Lord, that by abiding in the love of Christ we learn, at the school of Christ, the art of true love.

Follow me! In July 1958, the young priest Karol Wojtyla began a new stage in his journey with the Lord and in the footsteps of the Lord. Karol had gone to the Masuri lakes for his usual vacation, along with a group of young people who loved canoeing. But he brought with him a letter inviting him to call on the primate of Poland, Cardinal Wyszynski. He could guess the purpose of the meeting: He was to be appointed as the auxiliary bishop of Krakow.

Leaving the academic world, leaving this challenging engagement with young people, leaving the great intellectual endeavor of striving to understand and interpret the mystery of that creature which is man and of communicating to today's world the Christian interpretation of our being - all this must have seemed to him like losing his very self, losing what had become the very human identity of this young priest. Follow me - Karol Wojtyla accepted the appointment, for he heard in the Church's call the voice of Christ. And then he realized how true are the Lord's words: "Whoever seeks to preserve his life will lose it, but whoever loses it will save it" (*Luke* 17:33).

Our Pope - and we all know this - never wanted to make his own life secure, to keep it for himself; he wanted to give of himself unreservedly, to the very last moment, for Christ and thus also for us. And thus he came to experience how everything which he had given over into the Lord's hands, came back to him in a new way. His love of words, of poetry, of literature, became an essential part of his pastoral mission and gave new vitality, new urgency, new attractiveness to the preaching of the Gospel, even when it is a sign of contradiction.

Follow me! In October 1978, Cardinal Wojtyla once again heard the voice of the Lord. Once more there took place that dialogue with Peter reported in the Gospel of this Mass: "Simon, son of John, do you love me? Feed my sheep!" To the Lord's question, "Karol, do you love me?" the archbishop of Krakow answered from the depths of his heart: "Lord you know everything; you know that I love you." The love of Christ was the dominant force in the life of our beloved Holy Father. Anyone who ever saw him pray, who ever heard him preach, knows that. Thanks to his being profoundly rooted in Christ, he was able to bear a burden which transcends merely human abilities: that of being the shepherd of Christ's flock, his universal Church.

This is not the time to speak of the specific content of this rich pontificate. I would like only to read two passages of today's liturgy which reflect central elements of his message. In the first reading, St. Peter says - and with St. Peter, the Pope himself -

"In truth, I see that God shows no partiality. Rather, in every nation whoever fears him and acts uprightly is acceptable to him. You know the word (that) he sent to the Israelites as he proclaimed peace through Jesus Christ, who is Lord of all" (*Acts* 10:34-36). And in the second reading, St. Paul - and with St. Paul, our late Pope - exhorts us, crying out: "Therefore, my brothers, whom I love and long for, my joy and crown, in this way stand firm in the Lord, beloved" (*Phil* 4:1).

Follow me! Together with the command to feed his flock, Christ proclaimed to Peter that he would die a martyr's death. With those words, which conclude and sum up the dialogue on love and on the mandate of the universal shepherd, the Lord recalls another dialogue, which took place during the Last Supper. There Jesus had said: "Where I am going, you cannot come." Peter said to him, "Lord, where are you going?" Jesus replied: "Where I am going, you cannot follow me now; but you will follow me afterward" (*John* 13:33, 36). Jesus from the Supper went toward the Cross, went toward his resurrection - he entered into the paschal mystery; and Peter could not yet follow him. Now - after the resurrection - comes the time, comes this "afterward."

By shepherding the flock of Christ, Peter enters into the paschal mystery, he goes toward the cross and the resurrection. The Lord says this in these words: "when you were younger, you used to dress yourself and go where you wanted; but when you grow old, you will stretch out your hands, and someone else will dress you and lead you where you do not want to go" (*John* 21:18).

In the first years of his pontificate, still young and full of energy, the Holy Father went to the very ends of the earth, guided by Christ. But afterward, he increasingly entered into the communion of Christ's sufferings; increasingly he understood the truth of the words: "someone else will dress you." And in this very communion with the suffering Lord, tirelessly and with renewed intensity, he proclaimed the Gospel, the mystery of that love which goes to the end (cf. *John* 13:1).

He interpreted for us the paschal mystery as a mystery of divine mercy. In his last book, he wrote: The limit imposed upon evil "is ultimately Divine Mercy" ("*Memory and Identity*," pp. 60- 61). And reflecting on the assassination attempt, he said: "In sacrificing himself for us all, Christ gave a new meaning to suffering, opening up a new dimension, a new order: the order of love. ... It is this suffering which burns and consumes evil with the flame of love and draws forth even from sin a great flowering of good" (pp. 189-190). Impelled by this vision, the

Pope suffered and loved in communion with Christ, and that is why the message of his suffering and his silence proved so eloquent and so fruitful.

Divine Mercy: the Holy Father found the purest reflection of God's mercy in the Mother of God. He, who at an early age had lost his own mother, loved his divine mother all the more. He heard the words of the crucified Lord as addressed personally to him: "Behold your Mother." And so he did as the beloved disciple did: "he took her into his own home" (*John* 19:27) - "*Totus tuus.*" And from the mother he learned to conform himself to Christ.

None of us can ever forget how in that last Easter Sunday of his life, the Holy Father, marked by suffering, came once more to the window of the Apostolic Palace and one last time gave his blessing "urbi et orbi." We can be sure that our beloved Pope is standing today at the window of the Father's house, that he sees us and blesses us. Yes, bless us, Holy Father. We entrust your dear soul to the Mother of God, your Mother, who guided you each day and who will guide you now to the eternal glory of her Son, our Lord Jesus Christ. Amen.

2. Homily of His Eminence Cardinal Joseph Ratzinger, Dean of the College of Cardinals, during the Mass for the Election of the Roman Pontiff

Vatican Basilica, Monday 18 April 2005

At this moment of great responsibility, let us listen with special attention to what the Lord says to us in his own words. I would like to examine just a few passages from the three readings that concern us directly at this time.

The first one offers us a prophetic portrait of the person of the Messiah - a portrait that receives its full meaning from the moment when Jesus reads the text in the synagogue at Nazareth and says, "Today this Scripture passage is fulfilled in your hearing" (*Lk* 4:21).

At the core of the prophetic text we find a word which seems contradictory, at least at first sight. The Messiah, speaking of himself, says that he was sent "to announce a year of favour from the Lord and a day of vindication by our God" (*Is* 61:2). We hear with joy the news of a year of favour: divine mercy puts a limit on evil, as the Holy Father told us. Jesus Christ is divine mercy in person: encountering Christ means encountering God's mercy.

Christ's mandate has become our mandate through the priestly anointing. We are called to proclaim, not only with our words but also with our lives and with the valuable signs of the sacraments, "the year of favour from the Lord".

But what does the prophet Isaiah mean when he announces "the day of vindication by our God"? At Nazareth, Jesus omitted these words in his reading of the prophet's text; he concluded by announcing the year of favour. Might this have been the reason for the outburst of scandal after his preaching? We do not know.

In any case, the Lord offered a genuine commentary on these words by being put to death on the cross. St Peter says: "In his own body he brought your sins to the cross" (1 *Pt* 2:24). And St Paul writes in his Letter to the Galatians: "Christ has delivered us from the power of the law's curse by himself becoming a curse for us, as it is written, "Accursed is anyone who is hanged on a tree'. This happened so that through Christ Jesus the blessing bestowed on Abraham might descend on the Gentiles in Christ Jesus, thereby making it possible for us to receive the promised Spirit through faith" (*Gal* 3:13f.).

Christ's mercy is not a grace that comes cheap, nor does it imply the trivialization of evil. Christ carries the full weight of evil and all its destructive force in his body and in his soul. He burns and transforms evil in suffering, in the fire of his suffering love. The day of vindication and the year of favour converge in the Paschal Mystery, in the dead and Risen Christ. This is the vengeance of God: he himself suffers for us, in the person of his Son. The more deeply stirred we are by the Lord's mercy, the greater the solidarity we feel with his suffering - and we become willing to complete in our own flesh "what is lacking in the afflictions of Christ" (*Col* 1:24).

Let us move on to the second reading, the letter to the Ephesians. Here we see essentially three aspects: first of all, the ministries and charisms in the Church as gifts of the Lord who rose and ascended into heaven; then, the maturing of faith and the knowledge of the Son of God as the condition and content of unity in the Body of Christ; and lastly, our common participation in the growth of the Body of Christ, that is, the transformation of the world into communion with the Lord.

Let us dwell on only two points. The first is the journey towards "the maturity of Christ", as the Italian text says, simplifying it slightly. More precisely, in accordance with the Greek text, we should speak of the "measure of the fullness of Christ" that we are called to attain if we are to be true adults in the faith. We must not remain children in faith, in the condition of minors. And what does it mean to be children in faith? St Paul answers: it means being "tossed here and there, carried about by every wind of doctrine" (*Eph* 4:14). This description is very timely!

How many winds of doctrine have we known in recent decades, how many ideological currents, how many ways of thinking. The small boat of the thought of many Christians has often been tossed about by these waves - flung from one extreme to another: from Marxism to liberalism, even to libertinism;· from collectivism to radical individualism; from atheism to a vague religious mysticism; from agnosticism to syncretism and so forth. Every day new sects spring up, and what St Paul says about human deception and the trickery that strives to entice people into error (cf. *Eph* 4:14) comes true.

Today, having a clear faith based on the Creed of the Church is often labeled as fundamentalism. Whereas relativism, that is, letting oneself be "tossed here and there, carried about by every wind of doctrine", seems the only attitude that can cope with modern times. We are building a dictatorship of relativism that does not recognize anything as definitive and whose ultimate goal consists solely of one's own ego and desires.

We, however, have a different goal: the Son of God, the true man. He is the measure of true humanism. An "adult" faith is not a faith that follows the trends of fashion and the latest novelty; a mature adult faith is deeply rooted in friendship with Christ. It is this friendship that opens us up to all that is good and gives us a criterion by which to distinguish the true from the false, and deceipt from truth.

We must develop this adult faith; we must guide the flock of Christ to this faith. And it is this faith - only faith - that creates unity and is fulfilled in love.

On this theme, St Paul offers us as a fundamental formula for Christian existence some beautiful words, in contrast to the continual vicissitudes of those who, like children, are tossed about by the waves: make truth in love. Truth and love coincide in Christ. To the extent that we draw close to Christ, in our own lives too, truth and love are blended. Love without truth would be blind; truth without love would be like "a clanging cymbal" (1 7 13:1).

Let us now look at the Gospel, from whose riches I would like to draw only two small observations. The Lord addresses these wonderful words to us: "I no longer speak of you as slaves.... Instead, I call you friends" (*Jn* 15:15). We so often feel, and it is true, that we are only useless servants (cf. *Lk* 17:10).

Yet, in spite of this, the Lord calls us friends, he makes us his friends, he gives us his friendship. The Lord gives friendship a dual definition. There are no secrets between friends: Christ tells us all that he hears from the Father; he gives us his full trust and with trust, also knowledge. He reveals his face and his heart to us. He shows us the tenderness he feels for us, his passionate love that goes even as far as the folly of the Cross. He entrusts himself to us, he gives us the power to speak in his name: "this is my body...", "I forgive you...". He entrusts his Body, the Church, to us.

To our weak minds, to our weak hands, he entrusts his truth - the mystery of God the Father, the Son and the Holy Spirit; the mystery of God who "so loved the world that he gave his only Son" (*Jn* 3:16). He made us his friends - and how do we respond?

The second element Jesus uses to define friendship is the communion of wills. For the Romans "Idem velle - idem nolle" [same desires, same dislikes] was also the definition of friendship. "You are my friends if you do what I command you" (*Jn* 15:14). Friendship with Christ coincides with the third request of the Our Father: "Thy will be done on earth as it is in heaven". At his hour in the Garden of Gethsemane, Jesus transformed our rebellious human will into a will conformed and united with the divine will. He suffered the whole drama of our autonomy - and precisely by placing our will in God's hands, he gives us true freedom: "Not as I will, but as you will" (*Mt* 26:39).

Our redemption is brought about in this communion of wills: being friends of Jesus, to become friends of God. The more we love Jesus, the more we know him, the more our true freedom develops and our joy in being redeemed flourishes. Thank you, Jesus, for your friendship!

The other element of the Gospel to which I wanted to refer is Jesus' teaching on bearing fruit: "It was I who chose you to go forth and bear fruit. Your fruit must endure" (*Jn* 15:16).

It is here that appears the dynamism of the life of a Christian, an apostle: I chose you to go forth. We must be enlivened by a holy restlessness: a restlessness to bring to everyone the gift of faith, of friendship with Christ. Truly, the love and friendship of God was given to us so that it might also be shared with others. We have received the faith to give it to others - we are priests in order to serve others. And we must bear fruit that will endure.

All people desire to leave a lasting mark. But what endures? Money does not. Even buildings do not, nor books. After a certain time, longer or shorter, all these things disappear. The only thing that lasts for ever is the human soul, the human person created by God for eternity.

The fruit that endures is therefore all that we have sown in human souls: love, knowledge, a gesture capable of touching hearts, words that open the soul to joy in the Lord. So let us go and pray to the Lord to help us bear fruit that endures. Only in this way will the earth be changed from a valley of tears to a garden of God.

To conclude, let us return once again to the Letter to the Ephesians. The Letter says, with words from Psalm 68, that Christ, ascending into heaven, "gave gifts to men" (*Eph* 4:8). The victor offers gifts. And these gifts are apostles, prophets, evangelists, pastors and teachers. Our ministry is a gift of Christ to humankind, to build up his body - the new world. We live out our ministry in this way, as a gift of Christ to humanity!

At this time, however, let us above all pray insistently to the Lord that after his great gift of Pope John Paul II, he will once again give us a Pastor according to his own heart, a Pastor who will guide us to knowledge of Christ, to his love and to true joy. Amen.

3. Apostolic Blessing "Urbi et Orbi" Of His Holiness Benedict XVI

April 19, 2005

Dear Brothers and Sisters,

After the great Pope John Paul II, the Cardinals have elected me, a simple and humble labourer in the vineyard of the Lord.

The fact that the Lord knows how to work and to act even with inadequate instruments comforts me, and above all I entrust myself to your prayers.

Let us move forward in the joy of the Risen Lord, confident of his unfailing help. The Lord will help us and Mary, his Most Holy Mother, will be on our side. Thank you.

4. First Message of His Holiness Benedict XVI at the end of the Eucharistic Concelebration with the members of the College of Cardinals

The Sistine Chapel, Wednesday, 20 April 2005

Grace and peace in abundance to all of you! In my soul there are two contrasting sentiments in these hours. On the one hand, a sense of inadequacy and human turmoil for the responsibility entrusted to me yesterday as the Successor of the Apostle Peter in this See of Rome, with regard to the Universal Church. On the other hand I sense within me profound gratitude to God Who - as the liturgy makes us sing - does not abandon His flock, but leads it throughout time, under the guidance of those whom He has chosen as vicars of His Son, and made pastors.

Dear Ones, this intimate recognition for a gift of divine mercy prevails in my heart in spite of everything. I consider this a grace obtained for me by my venerated predecessor, John Paul II. It seems I can feel his strong hand squeezing mine; I seem to see his smiling eyes and listen to his words, addressed to me especially at this moment: 'Do not be afraid!'

The death of the Holy Father John Paul II, and the days which followed, were for the Church and for the entire world an extraordinary time of grace. The great pain for his death and the void that it left in all of us were tempered by the action of the Risen Christ, which showed itself during long days in the choral wave of faith, love and spiritual solidarity, culminating in his solemn funeral.

We can say it: the funeral of John Paul II was a truly extraordinary experience in which was perceived in some way the power of God Who, through His Church, wishes to form a great family of all peoples, through the unifying force of Truth and Love. In the hour of death, conformed to his Master and Lord, John Paul II crowned his long and fruitful pontificate, confirming the Christian people in faith, gathering them around him and making the entire human family feel more united.

How can one not feel sustained by this witness? How can one not feel the encouragement that comes from this event of grace?

Surprising every prevision I had, Divine Providence, through the will of the venerable Cardinal Fathers, called me to succeed this great Pope. I have been thinking in these hours about what happened in the region of Cesarea of Phillippi two thousand years ago: I seem to hear the words of

Peter: 'You are Christ, the Son of the living God,' and the solemn affirmation of the Lord: 'You are Peter and on this rock I will build my Church ... I will give you the keys of the kingdom of heaven'.

You are Christ! You are Peter! It seems I am reliving this very Gospel scene; I, the Successor of Peter, repeat with trepidation the anxious words of the fisherman from Galilee and I listen again with intimate emotion to the reassuring promise of the divine Master. If the weight of the responsibility that now lies on my poor shoulders is enormous, the divine power on which I can count is surely immeasurable: 'You are Peter and on this rock I will build my Church'. Electing me as the Bishop of Rome, the Lord wanted me as his Vicar, he wished me to be the 'rock' upon which everyone may rest with confidence. I ask him to make up for the poverty of my strength, that I may be a courageous and faithful pastor of His flock, always docile to the inspirations of His Spirit.

I undertake this special ministry, the 'Petrine' ministry at the service of the Universal Church, with humble abandon to the hands of the Providence of God. And it is to Christ in the first place that I renew my total and trustworthy adhesion: 'In Te, Domine, speravi; non confundar in aeternum!'

To you, Lord Cardinals, with a grateful soul for the trust shown me, I ask you to sustain me with prayer and with constant, active and wise collaboration. I also ask my brothers in the episcopacy to be close to me in prayer and counsel so that I may truly be the 'Servus servorum Dei' (Servant of the servants of God). As Peter and the other Apostles were, through the will of the Lord, one apostolic college, in the same way the Successor of Peter and the Bishops, successors of the Apostles - and the Council forcefully repeated this - must be closely united among themselves. This collegial communion, even in the diversity of roles and functions of the Supreme Pontiff and the bishops, is at the service of the Church and the unity of faith, from which depend in a notable measure the effectiveness of the evangelizing action of the contemporary world. Thus, this path, upon which my venerated predecessors went forward, I too intend to follow, concerned solely with proclaiming to the world the living presence of Christ.

Before my eyes is, in particular, the witness of Pope John Paul II. He leaves us a Church that is more courageous, freer, younger. A Church that, according to his teaching and example, looks with serenity to the past and is not afraid of the future. With the Great Jubilee the Church was introduced into the new millennium carrying in her hands the Gospel, applied to the world through the authoritative re-reading of Vatican Council II. Pope John Paul II justly indicated the Council as a 'compass' with which to orient ourselves in the vast ocean of the third millennium. Also in his spiritual testament he noted: ' I am convinced that for a very long time the new generations will draw upon the riches that this council of the 20th century gave us'.

I too, as I start in the service that is proper to the Successor of Peter, wish to affirm with force my decided will to pursue the commitment to enact Vatican Council II, in the wake of my predecessors and in faithful continuity with the millennia-old tradition of the Church. Precisely this year is the 40th anniversary of the conclusion of this conciliar assembly (December 8, 1965). With the passing of time, the conciliar documents have not lost their timeliness; their teachings have shown themselves to be especially pertinent to the new exigencies of the Church and the present globalized society.

In a very significant way, my pontificate starts as the Church is living the special year dedicated to the Eucharist. How can I not see in this providential coincidence an element that must mark the ministry to which I have been called? The Eucharist, the heart of Christian life and the source of the evangelizing mission of the Church, cannot but be the permanent center and the source of the petrine service entrusted to me.

The Eucharist makes the Risen Christ constantly present, Christ Who continues to give Himself to us, calling us to participate in the banquet of His Body and His Blood. From this full communion with Him comes every other element of the life of the Church, in the first place the communion among the faithful, the commitment to proclaim and give witness to the Gospel, the ardor of charity towards all, especially towards the poor and the smallest.

In this year, therefore, the Solemnity of Corpus Christ must be celebrated in a particularly special way. The Eucharist will be at the center, in August, of World Youth Day in Cologne and, in October, of the ordinary Assembly of the Synod of Bishops which will take place on the theme "The Eucharist, Source and Summit of the Life and Mission of the Church.' I ask everyone to intensify in coming months love and devotion to the Eucharistic Jesus and to express in a courageous and clear way the real presence of the Lord, above all through the solemnity and the correctness of the celebrations.

I ask this in a special way of priests, about whom I am thinking in this moment with great affection. The priestly ministry was born in the Cenacle, together with the Eucharist, as my venerated predecessor John Paul II underlined so many times. 'The priestly life must have in a special way a

'Eucharistic form', he wrote in his last Letter for Holy Thursday. The devout daily celebration of Holy Mass, the center of the life and mission of every priest, contributes to this end.

Nourished and sustained by the Eucharist, Catholics cannot but feel stimulated to tend towards that full unity for which Christ hoped in the Cenacle. Peter's Successor knows that he must take on this supreme desire of the Divine Master in a particularly special way. To him, indeed, has been entrusted the duty of strengthening his brethren.

Thus, in full awareness and at the beginning of his ministry in the Church of Rome that Peter bathed with his blood, the current Successor assumes as his primary commitment that of working tirelessly towards the reconstitution of the full and visible unity of all Christ's followers. This is his ambition, this is his compelling duty. He is aware that to do so, expressions of good feelings are not enough. Concrete gestures are required to penetrate souls and move consciences, encouraging everyone to that interior conversion which is the basis for all progress on the road of ecumenism.

Theological dialogue is necessary. A profound examination of the historical reasons behind past choices is also indispensable. But even more urgent is that 'purification of memory,' which was so often evoked by John Paul II, and which alone can dispose souls to welcome the full truth of Christ. It is before Him, supreme Judge of all living things, that each of us must stand, in the awareness that one day we must explain to Him what we did and what we did not do for the great good that is the full and visible unity of all His disciples.

The current Successor of Peter feels himself to be personally implicated in this question and is disposed to do all in his power to promote the fundamental cause of ecumenism. In the wake of his predecessors, he is fully determined to cultivate any initiative that may seem appropriate to promote contact and agreement with representatives from the various Churches and ecclesial communities. Indeed, on this occasion too, he sends them his most cordial greetings in Christ, the one Lord of all.

In this moment, I go back in my memory to the unforgettable experience we all underwent with the death and the funeral of the lamented John Paul II. Around his mortal remains, lying on the bare earth, leaders of nations gathered, with people from all social classes and especially the young, in an unforgettable embrace of affection and admiration. The entire world looked to him with trust. To many it seemed as if that intense participation, amplified to the confines of the planet by the social communications media, was like a choral request for help addressed to the Pope by modern humanity which, wracked by fear and uncertainty, questions itself about the future.

The Church today must revive within herself an awareness of the task to present the world again with the voice of the One Who said: 'I am the light of the world; he who follows me will not walk in darkness but will have the light of life.' In undertaking his ministry, the new Pope knows that his task is to bring the light of Christ to shine before the men and women of today: not his own light but that of Christ.

With this awareness, I address myself to everyone, even to those who follow other religions or who are simply seeking an answer to the fundamental questions of life and have not yet found it. I address everyone with simplicity and affection, to assure them that the Church wants to continue to build an open and sincere dialogue with them, in a search for the true good of mankind and of society.

From God I invoke unity and peace for the human family and declare the willingness of all Catholics to cooperate for true social development, one that respects the dignity of all human beings.

I will make every effort and dedicate myself to pursuing the promising dialogue that my predecessors began with various civilizations, because it is mutual understanding that gives rise to conditions for a better future for everyone.

I am particularly thinking of young people. To them, the privileged interlocutors of John Paul II, I send an affectionate embrace in the hope, God willing, of meeting them at Cologne on the occasion of the next World Youth Day. With you, dear young people, I will continue to maintain a dialogue, listening to your expectations in an attempt to help you meet ever more profoundly the living, ever young, Christ.

'Mane nobiscum, Domine!' Stay with us Lord! This invocation, which forms the dominant theme of John Paul II's Apostolic Letter for the Year of the Eucharist, is the prayer that comes spontaneously from my heart as I turn to begin the ministry to which Christ has called me. Like Peter, I too renew to Him my unconditional promise of faithfulness. He alone I intend to serve as I dedicate myself totally to the service of His Church.

In support of this promise, I invoke the maternal intercession of Mary Most Holy, in whose hands I place the present and the future of my person and of the Church. May the Holy Apostles Peter and Paul, and all the saints, also intercede.

With these sentiments I impart to you venerated brother cardinals, to those participating in this ritual, and to all those following to us by television and radio, a special and affectionate blessing.

5. Homily of His Holiness Benedict XVI during the Mass for the Inauguration of his Pontificate

St. Peter's Square, Sunday, 24 April 2005

Your Eminences, My dear Brother Bishops and Priests, Distinguished Authorities and Members of the Diplomatic Corps,Dear Brothers and Sisters,

During these days of great intensity, we have chanted the litany of the saints on three different occasions: at the funeral of our Holy Father John Paul II; as the Cardinals entered the Conclave; and again today, when we sang it with the response: Tu illum adiuva - sustain the new Successor of Saint Peter. On each occasion, in a particular way, I found great consolation in listening to this prayerful chant.

How alone we all felt after the passing of John Paul II - the Pope who for over twenty-six years had been our shepherd and guide on our journey through life! He crossed the threshold of the next life, entering into the mystery of God. But he did not take this step alone. Those who believe are never alone - neither in life nor in death. At that moment, we could call upon the Saints from every age - his friends, his brothers and sisters in the faith - knowing that they would form a living procession to accompany him into the next world, into the glory of God. We knew that his arrival was awaited. Now we know that he is among his own and is truly at home.

We were also consoled as we made our solemn entrance into Conclave, to elect the one whom the Lord had chosen. How would we be able to discern his name? How could 115 Bishops, from every culture and every country, discover the one on whom the Lord wished to confer the mission of binding and loosing? Once again, we knew that we were not alone, we knew that we were surrounded, led and guided by the friends of God. And now, at this moment, weak servant of God that I am, I must assume this enormous task, which truly exceeds all human capacity. How can I do this? How will I be able to do it? All of you, my dear friends, have just invoked the entire host of Saints, represented by some of the great names in the history of God's dealings with mankind. In this way, I too can say with renewed conviction: I am not alone. I do not have to carry alone what in truth I could never carry alone. All the Saints of God are there to protect me, to sustain me and to carry me. And your prayers, my dear friends, your indulgence, your love, your faith and your hope accompany me.

Indeed, the communion of Saints consists not only of the great men and women who went before us and whose names we know. All of us belong to the communion of Saints, we who have been baptized in the name of the Father, and of the Son and of the Holy Spirit, we who draw life from the gift of Christ's Body and Blood, through which he transforms us and makes us like himself. Yes, the Church is alive - this is the wonderful experience of these days. During those sad days of the Pope's illness and death, it became wonderfully evident to us that the Church is alive. And the Church is young. She holds within herself the future of the world and therefore shows each of us the way towards the future. The Church is alive and we are seeing it: we are experiencing the joy that the Risen Lord promised his followers. The Church is alive - she is alive because Christ is alive, because he is truly risen. In the suffering that we saw on the Holy Father's face in those days of Easter, we contemplated the mystery of Christ's Passion and we touched his wounds. But throughout these days we have also been able, in a profound sense, to touch the Risen One. We have been able to experience the joy that he promised, after a brief period of darkness, as the fruit of his resurrection.

The Church is alive - with these words, I greet with great joy and gratitude all of you gathered here, my venerable brother Cardinals and Bishops, my dear priests, deacons, Church workers, catechists. I greet you, men and women Religious, witnesses of the transfiguring presence of God. I greet you, members of the lay faithful, immersed in the great task of building up the Kingdom of God which spreads throughout the world, in every area of life. With great affection I also greet all those who have been reborn in the sacrament of Baptism but are not yet in full communion with us; and you, my brothers and sisters of the Jewish people, to whom we are joined by a great shared spiritual heritage, one rooted in God's irrevocable promises. Finally, like a wave gathering force, my thoughts go out to all men and women of today, to believers and non-believers alike.

Dear friends! At this moment there is no need for me to present a programme of governance. I was able to give an indication of what I see as my task in my Message of Wednesday 20 April, and there will be other opportunities to do so. My real programme of governance is not to do my own will, not to pursue my own ideas, but to listen, together with the whole Church, to the word and the will of the Lord, to be guided by Him, so that He himself will lead the Church at this hour of our history. Instead of putting forward a programme, I should simply like to comment on the two liturgical symbols which represent the inauguration of the Petrine Ministry; both these symbols, moreover, reflect clearly what we heard proclaimed in today's readings.

The first symbol is the Pallium, woven in pure wool, which will be placed on my shoulders. This ancient sign, which the Bishops of Rome have worn since the fourth century, may be considered an image of the yoke of Christ, which the Bishop of this City, the Servant of the Servants of God, takes upon his shoulders. God's yoke is God's will, which we accept. And this will does not weigh down on us, oppressing us and taking away our freedom. To know what God wants, to know where the path of life is found - this was Israel's joy, this was her great privilege. It is also our joy: God's will does not alienate us, it purifies us - even if this can be painful - and so it leads us to ourselves. In this way, we serve not only him, but the salvation of the whole world, of all history.

The symbolism of the Pallium is even more concrete: the lamb's wool is meant to represent the lost, sick or weak sheep which the shepherd places on his shoulders and carries to the waters of life. For the Fathers of the Church, the parable of the lost sheep, which the shepherd seeks in the desert, was an image of the mystery of Christ and the Church. The human race - every one of us - is the sheep lost in the desert which no longer knows the way. The Son of God will not let this happen; he cannot abandon humanity in so wretched a condition. He leaps to his feet and abandons the glory of heaven, in order to go in search of the sheep and pursue it, all the way to the Cross. He takes it upon his shoulders and carries our humanity; he carries us all - he is the good shepherd who lays down his life for the sheep.

What the Pallium indicates first and foremost is that we are all carried by Christ. But at the same time it invites us to carry one another. Hence the Pallium becomes a symbol of the shepherd's mission, of which the Second Reading and the Gospel speak. The pastor must be inspired by Christ's holy zeal: for him it is not a matter of indifference that so many people are living in the desert. And there are so many kinds of desert. There is the desert of poverty, the desert of hunger and thirst, the desert of abandonment, of loneliness, of destroyed love. There is the desert of God's darkness, the emptiness of souls no longer aware of their dignity or the goal of human life. The external deserts in the world are growing, because the internal deserts have become so vast. Therefore the earth's treasures no longer serve to build God's garden for all to live in, but they have been made to serve the powers of exploitation and destruction. The Church as a whole and all her Pastors, like Christ, must set out to lead people out of the desert, towards the place of life, towards friendship with the Son of God, towards the One who gives us life, and life in abundance.

The symbol of the lamb also has a deeper meaning. In the Ancient Near East, it was customary for kings to style themselves shepherds of their people. This was an image of their power, a cynical image: to them their subjects were like sheep, which the shepherd could dispose of as he wished. When the shepherd of all humanity, the living God, himself became a lamb, he stood on the side of the lambs, with those who are downtrodden and killed. This is how he reveals himself to be the true shepherd: "I am the Good Shepherd . . . I lay down my life for the sheep", Jesus says of himself (Jn 10:14f). It is not power, but love that redeems us! This is God's sign: he himself is love. How often we wish that God would make show himself stronger, that he would strike decisively, defeating evil and creating a better world. All ideologies of power justify themselves in exactly this way, they justify the destruction of whatever would stand in the way of progress and the liberation of humanity. We suffer on account of

God's patience. And yet, we need his patience. God, who became a lamb, tells us that the world is saved by the Crucified One, not by those who crucified him. The world is redeemed by the patience of God. It is destroyed by the impatience of man.

One of the basic characteristics of a shepherd must be to love the people entrusted to him, even as he loves Christ whom he serves. "Feed my sheep", says Christ to Peter, and now, at this moment, he says it to me as well. Feeding means loving, and loving also means being ready to suffer. Loving means giving the sheep what is truly good, the nourishment of God's truth, of God's word, the nourishment of his presence, which he gives us in the Blessed Sacrament. My dear friends - at this moment I can only say: pray for me, that I may learn to love the Lord more and more. Pray for me, that I may learn to love his flock more and more - in other words, you, the holy Church, each one of you and all of you together. Pray for me, that I may not flee for fear of the wolves. Let us pray for one another, that the Lord will carry us and that we will learn to carry one another.

The second symbol used in today's liturgy to express the inauguration of the Petrine Ministry is the presentation of the fisherman's ring. Peter's call to be a shepherd, which we heard in the Gospel, comes after the account of a miraculous catch of fish: after a night in which the disciples had let down their nets without success, they see the Risen Lord on the shore. He tells them to let down their nets once more, and the nets become so full that they can hardly pull them in; 153 large fish: "and although there were so many, the net was not torn" (Jn 21:11). This account, coming at the end of Jesus's earthly journey with his disciples, corresponds to an account found at the beginning: there too, the disciples had caught nothing the entire night; there too, Jesus had invited Simon once more to put out into the deep. And Simon, who was not yet called Peter, gave the wonderful reply: "Master, at your word I will let down the nets." And then came the conferral of his mission: "Do not be afraid. Henceforth you will be catching men" (*Lk* 5:1-11).

Today too the Church and the successors of the Apostles are told to put out into the deep sea of history and to let down the nets, so as to win men and women over to the Gospel - to God, to Christ, to true life. The Fathers made a very significant commentary on this singular task. This is what they say: for a fish, created for water, it is fatal to be taken out of the sea, to be removed from its vital element to serve as human food. But in the mission of a fisher of men, the reverse is true. We are living in alienation, in the salt waters of suffering and death; in a sea of darkness without light. The net of the Gospel pulls us out of the waters of death and brings us into the splendour of God's light, into true life.

It is really true: as we follow Christ in this mission to be fishers of men, we must bring men and women out of the sea that is salted with so many forms of alienation and onto the land of life, into the light of God. It is really so: the purpose of our lives is to reveal God to men. And only where God is seen does life truly begin. Only when we meet the living God in Christ do we know what life is. We are not some casual and meaningless product of evolution. Each of us is the result of a thought of God. Each of us is willed, each of us is loved, each of us is necessary. There is nothing more beautiful than to be surprised by the Gospel, by the encounter with Christ. There is nothing more beautiful than to know Him and to speak to others of our friendship with Him. The task of the shepherd, the task of the fisher of men, can often seem wearisome. But it is beautiful and wonderful, because it is truly a service to joy, to God's joy which longs to break into the world.

Here I want to add something: both the image of the shepherd and that of the fisherman issue an explicit call to unity. "I have other sheep that are not of this fold; I must lead them too, and they will heed my voice. So there shall be one flock, one shepherd" (Jn 10:16); these are the words of Jesus at the end of his discourse on the Good Shepherd. And the account of the 153 large fish ends with the joyful statement: "although there were so many, the net was not torn" (*Jn* 21:11). Alas, beloved Lord, with sorrow we must now acknowledge that it has been torn! But no - we must not be sad! Let us rejoice because of your promise, which does not disappoint, and let us do all we can to pursue the path towards the unity you have promised. Let us remember it in our prayer to the Lord, as we plead with him: yes, Lord, remember your promise. Grant that we may be one flock and one shepherd! Do not allow your net to be torn, help us to be servants of unity!

At this point, my mind goes back to 22 October 1978, when Pope John Paul II began his ministry here in Saint Peter's Square. His words on that occasion constantly echo in my ears: "Do not be afraid! Open wide the doors for Christ!" The Pope was addressing the mighty, the powerful of this world, who feared that Christ might take away something of their power if they were to let him in, if they were to allow the faith to be free. Yes, he would certainly have taken something away from them: the dominion of corruption, the manipulation of law and the freedom to do as they pleased. But he would not have taken away anything that pertains to human freedom or dignity, or to the building of a just society.

The Pope was also speaking to everyone, especially the young. Are we not perhaps all afraid in some way? If we let Christ enter fully into our lives, if we open ourselves totally to him, are we not afraid that He might take something away from us? Are we not perhaps afraid to give up something significant, something unique, something that makes life so beautiful? Do we not then risk ending up diminished and deprived of our freedom? And once again the Pope said: No! If we let Christ into our lives, we lose nothing, nothing, absolutely nothing of what makes life free, beautiful and great. No! Only in this friendship are the doors of life opened wide. Only in this friendship is the great potential of human existence truly revealed. Only in this friendship do we experience beauty and liberation. And so, today, with great strength and great conviction, on the basis of long personal experience of life, I say to you, dear young people: Do not be afraid of Christ! He takes nothing away, and he gives you everything. When we give ourselves to him, we receive a hundredfold in return. Yes, open, open wide the doors to Christ - and you will find true life. Amen.

6. Homily of His Holiness Benedict XVI when visiting the Sepulchre of the Apostle to the Gentiles

Basilica of St. Paul Outside the Walls, 25 April 2005

Lord Cardinals
Venerated Brothers in the Episcopate and in the Priesthood
Dear Brothers and Sisters:

I thank God because at the beginning of my ministry as Successor of Peter he grants me to pause in prayer before the sepulchre of the Apostle Paul. For me, this is a much longed for pilgrimage, a gesture of faith that I make in my name, but also in the name of the beloved Diocese of Rome, of which the Lord has constituted me Bishop and Pastor, and of the universal Church entrusted to my pastoral care. A pilgrimage so to speak to the roots of the mission, of that mission that the risen Christ entrusted to Peter, to the Apostles and, in particular also to Paul, leading him to proclaim the Gospel to the Gentiles, until he reached this city where, after having preached the Kingdom of God for a long time (*Acts* 28:31), he rendered with blood the last testimony of his Lord, who had "made him his own" (*Philippians* 3:12) and sent him.

Already before Providence led him to Rome, the Apostle wrote to the Christians of this city, capital of the Empire, his most important letter from the doctrinal point of view. Its beginning has just been proclaimed, a profound preamble in which the Apostle greets the community of Rome introducing himself as "servant of Jesus Christ, called to be an Apostle" (*Romans* 1:1). And later he adds: "through [Jesus Christ] we have received grace and apostleship to bring about the obedience of faith for the sake of his name among all the nations" (*Romans* 1:5).

Dear Friends, as Successor of Peter, I am here to revive in faith this "grace of apostleship," as God, according to another expression of the Apostle to the Gentiles, has entrusted to me "anxiety for all the churches" (*2 Corinthians* 11:28). Before our eyes is the example of my beloved and venerated predecessor John Paul II, a missionary Pope whose activity, understood in this way, witnessed in more than 100 apostolic trips beyond the confines of Italy, is truly inimitable. What was it that drove him to such dynamism if not the very love of Christ that transformed St. Paul's life (cf. *2 Corinthians* 5:14)? May the Lord infuse such a love also in me so that I will not remain calm in face of the urgencies of the proclamation of the Gospel in today's world. The Church by her nature is missionary; her primary task is evangelization. The ecumenical Second Vatican Council dedicated to missionary activity the decree called precisely, "Ad Gentes," in which we are reminded that "[t]he Apostles themselves, on whom the Church was founded, following in the footsteps of Christ, 'preached the word of truth and begot churches.' It is the duty of their successors to make this task endure 'so that the word of God may run and be glorified (*2 Thessalonians* 3:1) and the kingdom of God be proclaimed and established throughout the world."

At the beginning of the third millennium, the Church feels with renewed force that Christ's missionary mandate is of more current importance than ever. The Great Jubilee of the Year 2000 has led her to "start afresh from Christ," contemplated in prayer, so that the light of his truth is irradiated to all men, above all with the testimony of holiness. I like to recall the motto that St. Benedict proposed in his Rule, when exhorting his monks to "prefer nothing to the love of Christ" (Chapter 4). In fact, the call on the road to Damascus led Paul precisely to this: to make Christ the center of his life, leaving everything for the sublime knowledge of him and of his ministry of love, committing himself later to proclaim him to all, especially pagans "to the glory of his name" (Romans 1:5). Christ's passion led him to preach the Gospel not only with the word, but also with his very life, which was ever more conformed to that of his Lord. In the end, Paul proclaimed Christ with martyrdom, and his blood, together with that of Peter and of witnesses of the Gospel, watered this land and made fruitful the Church of Rome, which presides over the communion of charity (cf. St. Ignatius of Antioch, "Letter to the Romans," 1,1).

The 20th century was a time of martyrdom. Pope John Paul II highlighted it clearly, asking the Church to "actualize the Martyrology" and canonized and beatified numerous martyrs of recent history. Therefore, the blood of martyrs is the seed of new Christians, especially there where it has suffered most for the faith and the testimony of the Gospel.

We entrust this desire to the intercession of St. Paul. May he obtain for the Church of Rome, in particular for her Bishop, and for all the people of God, the joy of proclaiming and witnessing to all the Good News of Christ the Saviour.

7. Why the name 'Benedict'?

I wished to call myself Benedict XVI to be united ideally with the venerated Pontiff Benedict XV, who led the Church in a troubled time because of World War I. He was a courageous and authentic prophet of peace and he did his utmost with strenuous courage from the start to avoid the drama of the war and then to limit its inauspicious consequences. Following his footsteps, I wish to put my ministry at the service of reconciliation and harmony among men and nations, profoundly convinced that the great good of peace is, first of all, a gift of God, a fragile and precious gift to be invoked, defended and built day after day with the contribution of all.

The name Benedict evokes, moreover, the extraordinary figure of the great "patriarch of Western monasticism," St. Benedict of Nursia, co-patron of Europe together with Saints Cyril and Methodius. The gradual expansion of the Benedictine Order founded by him has had an enormous influence on the spread of Christianity on the whole Continent. Because of this, St. Benedict is much venerated in Germany and, in particular, in Bavaria, my native land. He constitutes a fundamental point of reference for the unity of Europe and a strong reminder of the inalienable Christian roots of its culture and its civilization.

We know the recommendation left to his monks in his Rule by this Father of Western monasticism: "Prefer absolutely nothing to Christ" (Rule 72,11; cf. 4,21). At the beginning of my service as Successor of Peter I pray to St. Benedict to help us to hold firm the centrality of Christ in our life. May he always be first in our thoughts and in all our activity!

(*First General Audience, St. Peter's Square, 27 April 2005*).

Biographical note

Cardinal Joseph Ratzinger, former prefect of the Congregation for the Doctrine of the Faith, President of the Pontifical Biblical Commission and of the International Theological Commission, Dean of the College of Cardinals, was born on April 16, 1927 in Marktl am Inn, Germany. He was ordained a priest on June 29, 1951.

His father, a police officer, came from a traditional family of farmers from Lower Bavaria. He spent his adolescent years in Traunstein, and was called into the auxiliary anti-aircraft service in the last months of World War II. From 1946 to 1951, the year in which he was ordained a priest and began to teach, he studied philosophy and theology at the University of Munich and at the higher school in Freising. In 1953 he obtained a doctorate in theology with a thesis entitled: *"The People and House of God in St. Augustine's doctrine of the Church."* Four years later, he qualified as a university teacher. He then taught dogma and fundamental theology at the higher school of philosophy and theology of Freising, in Bonn from 1959 to 1969, in Munster from 1963 to 1966, and in Tubinga from 1966 to 1969. From 1969, he was professor of dogmatic theology and of the history of dogma at the University of Regensburg and vice president of the same university.

He was already well known in 1962 when, at Vatican Council II at the age of 35, he became a consultor to Cardinal Joseph Frings, archbishop of Cologne. Among his numerous publications, a particular post belongs to the "Introduction to Christianity," a collection of university lessons on the profession of apostolic faith, published in 1968; and to "Dogma and Revelation" an anthology of essays, sermons and reflections dedicated to the pastoral ministry, published in 1973.

In March 1977, Paul VI appointed him Archbishop of Munich and Freising and on May 28, 1977 he was consecrated - the first diocesan priest after 80 years to take over the pastoral ministry of this large Bavarian diocese. Created and proclaimed cardinal by Paul VI in the consistory of June 27, 1977, he assumed the titles of the suburbicarian Church of Velletri-Segni (April 5, 1993) and of the suburbicarian Church of Ostia (November 30, 2002). On November 25, 1981 he was nominated by John Paul II as prefect of the Congregation for the Doctrine of the Faith; and as president of the Biblical Commission and of the Pontifical International Theological Commission.

He was relator of the 5th General Assembly of the Synod of Bishops (1980). He was president delegate to the 6th Synodal Assembly (1983). Elected vice dean of the College of Cardinals November 6, 1998, the Holy Father approved his election, by the order of cardinal bishops, as dean of the College of Cardinals on November 30, 2002.

As President of the Commission for the Preparation of the Catechism of the Catholic Church, after 6 years of work (1986-92) he presented the New Catechism to the Holy Father. He received an honoris causa degree in jurisprudence from the Free University of Maria Santissima Assunta on November 10. 1999. He became an honorary member of the Pontifical Academy of Sciences, November 13, 2000.

His Curial Memberships have included Secretariat of State (second section); Oriental Churches, Divine Worship and Discipline of the Sacraments, Bishops, Evangelization of Peoples, Catholic Education (congregations); Christian Unity (council); Latin America, Ecclesia Dei (commissions).

He was elected Pope in the Conclave of Cardinals on 19 February 2005, three days after his 78th birthday.

Pope Benedict XVI's published works

Catholics are greatly blessed in our Holy Father, Pope Benedict XVI. One of the many reasons to be thankful is his remarkable stature as a writer and theologian. It is difficult to do more than hint at the richness of his published work, all of which shows the luminous quality of thought, and the prayerful sense of the Church's deep Tradition so evident in the wonderful homilies which he gave at the funeral of Pope John Paul II, before the Conclave, and at his inaugural Mass.

As is well known, before he was appointed to head the Congregation for the Doctrine of the Faith, he was prominent in the theological world of German universities. There, and during his time as a *peritus* (theological expert) at the Second Vatican Council, he was immersed in the profound tradition of the best twentieth century theology: Hans Urs von Balthasar and Henri de Lubac were personal mentors. His earliest well-known work is his *Introduction to Christianity* (1968), a commentary on the Apostle's Creed in the light of modern theology, especially of the great rediscovery of the Church Fathers that is the enduring legacy of theologians such as Balthasar and Lubac.

When he was appointed Prefect of the Congregation for the Doctrine of the Faith, Cardinal Ratzinger, as he then was, particularly asked that he be permitted to continue publishing his own works of theology; he has done so with astonishing frequency. Notable are two books based on interviews with the German journalist Peter Seewald: *Salt of the Earth* (1996), and *God and the World* (2000). These give an excellent and tremendously lucid survey of his thought on a whole range of topics central to Christianity today, and are all the more impressive for being essentially spontaneous and unscripted.

In other books he has addressed particular questions: *Truth and Tolerance* (2004) examines Christianity's relation to other world religions, and to a society that typically denies any notion that truth can be found anywhere; *Called to Communion* (1996) looks at the nature of the Church today.

The Spirit of the Liturgy (2000) is a magnificent reflection on the nature and form of Christian worship, the place where God meets us; liturgy and especially the Mass is also the subject of *Feast of Faith* (1986), *A New Song for the Lord* (1996), and *God is Near Us* (2003). *Behold the Pierced One* (1987) relates Christian prayer to the fundamental reality of the Death and Resurrection of Christ; *Many Religions, One Covenant* (1999) examines the enduring nature of God's promises to the Jewish people. He was of course instrumental in the new *Catechism of the Catholic Church*: his book *Gospel, Catechesis, Catechism* (1997) grew out of this.

On a more personal level, *Milestones* (1998) is a delightful and moving memoir of his first fifty years, including his childhood in Bavaria during the Nazi period. Other titles include:

The Ratzinger Report (1985)
Principles of Christian Morality (1986) (co-written with Hans Urs von Balthasar)
Principles of Catholic Theology (1987)
Church, Ecumenism, and Politics (1988)
Eschatology (1989)
Ministers of Your Joy (1989)
In the Beginning (1990)
To Look on Christ (1991)
Co-Workers of the Truth (1992)
The Meaning of Christian Brotherhood (1993)
Turning Point for Europe (1994)
An Introduction to the Catechism (1994) (co-written with Cardinal Schönborn)
The Nature and Mission of Theology (1995)
The End of Time? (2005)
Pilgrim Fellowship of Faith (2005)

Informative Catholic Reading

We hope that you have enjoyed reading this booklet.

If you would like to find out more about CTS booklets - we'll send you our free information pack and catalogue.

Please send us your details:

Name ....

Address ....

....

....

Postcode ....

Telephone..

Email ....

Send to: CTS, 40-46 Harleyford Road,
            Vauxhall, London
            SE11 5AY

Tel: 020 7640 0042
Fax: 020 7640 0046
Email: info@cts-online.org.uk

Give yourself to Christ

First Homilies of Benedict XVI

The passing of one Pope and the election of a successor are events that combine to form a momentous few weeks in the life of the Catholic Church - and, as the events of April 2005 have illustrated, even beyond to a wider audience. The death of Pope John Paul II and the election of Pope Benedict XVI have certainly raised the interest of millions around the globe.

This collection of the homilies given by Cardinal Joseph Ratzinger during the period between the death of John Paul II, and his own election and inauguration as Pope Benedict XVI, capture the sentiments and aspirations not only of one man, or of the College of Cardinals, but the aspirations and prayers of a whole people.

ISBN 1-86082-337-8

9 781860 823374

CTS

D 675   £1.95